Stoicism

for Inner Peace
and Confidence

The Ultimate Guide to Stoicism

with a 90-Day Journal

Charles Abbott

Disclaimer

This book and its contents are provided for educational purposes only and are not intended to replace or substitute any professional, medical, legal, or any other advice. The content contained herein presents the philosophy of Stoicism and is intended for educational purposes only.

While there are discussions related to coping with mental health, health issues, and other life challenges, these are based on philosophical contemplation and personal insights from the perspective of Stoicism and should not be interpreted as medical, health, or psychological advice. If readers are facing medical conditions, mental health struggles, or personal crises, they are strongly encouraged to seek advice from qualified healthcare professionals or licensed therapists. The author and publisher specifically disclaim any responsibility for any liability, loss, or risk, personal or otherwise, that is incurred as a consequence, directly or indirectly, of the use and application of any of the contents of this book.

The author and publisher are not healthcare or mental health professionals, and the content presented should not be considered as medical or professional advice. The author and publisher are not liable for any errors, omissions, or inaccuracies in the content, or for any actions taken in reliance thereon. Furthermore, while the author has made every effort to ensure the accuracy and completeness of the information contained in this book, we apologize for any errors, omissions, or inconsistencies. Under no circumstances shall the author or publisher be liable for any special, direct, indirect, consequential, or incidental damages or any damages whatsoever, whether in an action of contract, negligence, or other torts, arising out of or in connection with the use of the content in this book. By continuing to read this book, you acknowledge and agree that you have fully understood this disclaimer and agree to use the information contained herein at your own risk and discretion.

Your Stoic Journey Supports Children in Need

In the pages that follow, not only will you embark on a journey of wonderful inner transformation and personal growth, but you will also be extending a hand of hope to children.

Our Commitment to Giving

This book is more than a literary endeavor; it is a heartfelt commitment to helping underprivileged children. **100% of the profits** from Charlie's books are donated directly to charitable efforts dedicated to **helping children in need.**

Charles Abbott's books are published by Mei Service, a boutique publishing house with a vision to help children to learn one word, and one book at a time.

Join Us

To learn more about our initiatives and how your contribution is lighting up young lives, we welcome you to visit us at: www.meiservicebooks.com

Embark on a journey of wisdom, knowing that your path through these pages helps pave the way for a brighter tomorrow for the young ones we serve. Together, let's turn the act of reading into a legacy of hope.

Sign up for updates:

https://subscribepage.io/stoicupdates

Contents

Your FREE Gift!

Get your **free 90-Day Stoic Journal**:

https://subscribepage.io/90daystoicjournal

Introduction

The Stoic Path to a Happy, Fulfilling Life

In the relentless hustle and bustle of today's world, many find themselves adrift, searching for a sense of purpose and meaning amidst the cacophony of life's demands.

The constant pressure to achieve, to fit in, and to meet societal expectations can erode our peace of mind, leaving us feeling overwhelmed, stressed, depressed, and disconnected from our true selves.

We grapple with self-doubt, face challenges that test our emotional fortitude, and yearn for a sanctuary of calm and clarity.

If you've ever felt this way, if you've ever sought a refuge from the storms of life and a roadmap to a more centered, joyful existence, then this book holds the solution for you.

In the ever-evolving landscape of the modern world, where the pursuit of happiness often feels like an elusive dream, the ancient philosophy of Stoicism provides a beacon of hope.

Stoicism, a philosophy rooted in the wisdom of the ancients, offers the antidote to our modern malaises.

If you find yourself meandering unhappily through life, seeking a clearer direction and the secret to living joyfully, Stoicism holds the map you need.

If you grapple with shaky confidence, yearn for strength, and crave resilience to face the world, the teachings of Stoicism will fortify your spirit.

And for those moments when life's challenges—trauma, anxiety, anger, overwhelming work fatigue, or the profound introspection of a mid-life crisis threaten to topple you, Stoicism offers both a shield and a guiding light.

Through Stoic skills and meditations, you'll find the path to sustained serenity and genuine happiness.

This book is not just an exploration of a historical ideology; it is a practical guide tailored for individuals like you, those who seek inner peace, unyielding confidence, emotional resilience, unwavering perseverance, deep-seated serenity, and a profound self-knowledge to cultivate a life of happiness and contentment.

Through its pages, you will find tools and teachings designed to address your pain points, alleviate your struggles, and usher you into a realm of Stoic tranquility.

Stoicism, with its rich history, profound teachings, and practical applications, offers individuals a structured path towards attaining inner peace, self-confidence, and a fulfilling life.

This book is your comprehensive guide to understanding and embracing the Stoic way of life.

Stoicism is not merely a set of esoteric teachings from bygone eras; it is a living, breathing philosophy that has been passed down through generations. From its inception in the bustling heart of Ancient Greece, it was propagated by revered teachers who not only preached its virtues but lived by them.

This book delves into the history of Stoicism, shedding light on its prominent teachers, its virtues, disciplines, and core beliefs that have inspired millions over centuries.

But Stoicism is not confined to the dusty pages of history. The modern world, with all its complexities, provides a fertile ground for the application of Stoic principles.

This book will show you how contemporary individuals apply Stoic philosophy in their everyday lives, navigating challenges with grace, resilience, and serenity. Moreover, you will discover the myriad Stoic skills that can help you take control of your mental and emotional life, enabling you to face life's adversities with a calm mind and a steadfast spirit.

One of this book's unique offerings is the 90-day Stoic journal—a practical guide designed to immerse you in Stoic meditation.

Through consistent practice, this journal promises to usher in a transformative journey, one where you will cultivate inner peace, unwavering confidence, emotional resilience, perseverance, and an enriched self-awareness.

As you turn its pages, day after day, you will find yourself increasingly aligned with the Stoic way, drawing from its wisdom to lead a harmonious life.

This book is also replete with powerful quotes and historic anecdotes that serve as both inspiration and reflection. They echo the timeless truths of Stoicism, reminding you of its enduring relevance.

So, if you find yourself asking questions like: "What is Stoicism?", "How can I lead a happy life?", "How can Stoic principles bolster my confidence and inner peace?", or "How can Stoicism guide me through life's tumultuous waves?", then you are in the right place.

You are holding the answers in your hands.

This book seeks to answer these and many other questions, providing you with tools, insights, and practices to imbue your life with the essence of Stoicism.

Embark on this enlightening journey with Stoicism as your compass, and let its teachings guide you to a life of contentment, inner peace, calmness, resilience, and profound joy.

How Stoicism Changed My Life

I found Stoicism during the lowest point of my life, and it profoundly changed everything.

For over a decade and a half, I battled the incessant demons of anxiety, coupled with relentless waves of depression. Neither the numbing comfort of anti-depressants nor the unraveling sessions of therapy provided any lasting relief nor significantly anchored my drifting spirit.

The onset of the COVID pandemic further escalated my internal turmoil, manifesting in frequent bouts of anxiety attacks, leaving me feeling helplessly adrift in a sea of uncertainty, fear, anger, and frustration.

This downward spiral continued, unabated. Personal tragedies and familial challenges stormed into my life uninvited — the devastating experience of my wife's miscarriage, the heartache accompanying our beloved daughter Melissa's autism diagnosis, and the looming shadow of financial ruin threatening my business.

Nights transformed into extended periods of insomnia, with stress clouding my mind and a restlessness twisting my soul.

However, life, in its mysterious ways, brought Stoicism to me through an old classmate's recommendation. Initially dismissive due to my indifference towards philosophy, the escalating chaos eventually propelled me towards this ancient wisdom.

The profundity of the first few Stoic tenets I encountered struck a chord so deep that it reverberated through the very core of my being, illuminating reasons behind the disarray in my life and the source of my incessant stress.

I found myself hungrily delving into every available manuscript and article on Stoicism, emerging after a year, not as a scholar, but as a practitioner fortified with tools to counter life's adversities.

The transformation was profound. Stoic practices equipped me to intercept an anxious thought, mitigate rising stress, or navigate emotional turbulence with such efficacy that an unparalleled tranquility enveloped me.

I learned to see my path as part of a larger tapestry, intricately woven for my personal journey toward growth. I developed an unshakable sense of reassurance, a conviction that, despite contrary appearances, I was treading the path charted by Destiny for my ultimate well-being.

Embracing Stoicism has been transformative.

Today, I stand as a beacon of stability for my children, exuding the calmness and reliability of a nurturing father.

My relationships have been tremendously improved, which is evident in my interactions with my family, friends, and professional acquaintances.

Gone are the oppressive, stormy clouds that once loomed over me, replaced now by the warmth and brightness of clarity and strength.

Even when life's inevitable tempests make their presence known, I remain unflinchingly resilient, my inner light a constant flame, undeterred by life's capricious nature.

Fears that once haunted me, whether of death, uncertainty, or loss, have dissolved – replaced by a newfound fortitude.

This inner metamorphosis has manifested externally. Circumstances or individuals no longer hold the power to perturb my peace.

Life feels brighter, balanced, and even when challenges arise. I'm fortified with inner resilience. My perspective has shifted. The external factors that once dictated my happiness no longer have that power.

This deep, internal change has brought genuine contentment. Daily frustrations or unforeseen difficulties don't shake my tranquility.

The Stoic principles I've assimilated grant me the strength to maintain courage and composure in the face of adversity — be it a conversation with a rude individual, confronting the mundane frustrations of everyday life, or soothing Melissa during her distressing episodes.

I can honestly say I've discovered the more priceless treasure of all – the secret to authentic inner contentment, peace, and joy.

Now, dear reader, this is the treasure I wish to share with you. Within these pages lie the practical, life-changing tools and exercises that have not only changed my life but also empowered millions globally to extract the nectar of life, savoring each day to its fullest potential.

This is not just philosophy. It's a daily practice, a journey towards true peace and contentment.

You'll discover the profound stability and joy that comes from within, regardless of life's storms.

Embark on this transformative journey with me, and I promise, the destination is nothing short of enlightenment and peace.

Bon voyage!

PART I

History of Stoicism

Stoicism, an influential school of ancient philosophy, has its roots deeply embedded in the Hellenistic period, offering profound insights on ethics, logic, and the natural world. Its teachings have transcended time, providing guidance for both ancient statesmen and modern-day individuals seeking purpose and tranquility amidst life's challenges.

Origins and Founding

The inception of Stoicism can be traced back to Athens around 300 BCE. The school owes its name to the Stoa Poikile, or "Painted Porch", a public colonnade where its founder, Zeno of Citium, began teaching his philosophy.

Zeno, originally a wealthy merchant, turned to philosophy after he was plunged into poverty when a shipwreck lost all of his cargo.

He studied under various philosophers, but it was his own synthesis of these teachings that led to the birth of Stoicism.

Key Figures

After Zeno, Stoicism's torch was passed to a series of notable thinkers:

- **Cleanthes**, Zeno's immediate successor, made significant contributions, particularly his hymn to Zeus, which encapsulates the Stoic belief in a rational and providential cosmos.

- **Chrysippus**, another early Stoic, was instrumental in developing the school's doctrines, especially in logic and ethics. His works, though largely lost, formed the foundation for many Stoic teachings.

In Rome, Stoicism found a new audience and several noteworthy proponents:

- **Seneca**, an advisor to Emperor Nero, authored numerous essays and letters elucidating Stoic principles, emphasizing the idea that virtue is the only true good.

- **Epictetus**, born a slave and later freed, focused on the dichotomy of control, teaching that one should concern oneself only with what one can control.

- **Marcus Aurelius**, the Roman Emperor, penned "Meditations", a series of personal notes that offer a window into his Stoic beliefs and practices.

Marcus Aurelius - Photo by Pierre-Selim

Evolution and Influence

While Stoicism's core teachings remained relatively consistent, its popularity ebbed and flowed.

It found fertile ground in Rome, especially during the tumultuous periods of the late Republic and early Empire. Here, Stoicism provided guidance on leading a virtuous life in a world rife with political unrest and moral decay.

However, with the rise of Christianity in the Roman Empire, Stoicism's influence began to wane.

Medieval Era: Stoicism and Christianity

After the fall of the Roman Empire, Stoicism saw a decline in popularity as it was largely overshadowed by the rise of Christianity. However, the two weren't entirely at odds.

Early Christian thinkers, such as Augustine, often incorporated Stoic ideas, especially those related to virtue and ethics.

The Stoic idea of the "Logos" found parallels in Christian theology, leading to a subtle fusion of certain Stoic and Christian beliefs.

Renaissance: Rediscovery and Reinterpretation

The Renaissance, with its renewed interest in classical texts, saw a revival of Stoic philosophy. Thinkers of the era, eager to reconcile classical knowledge with Christian beliefs, delved into Stoic texts. Erasmus, for instance, translated works of Seneca, reintroducing Stoic ideas to a wider audience.

This period saw Stoicism not as a competing philosophy, but rather as a complementary one, offering insights on personal ethics and virtue.

Enlightenment: Stoicism and Rationalism

The Age of Enlightenment, with its emphasis on reason and individual rights, found an ally in Stoicism.

Philosophers such as Immanuel Kant and John Locke, while not strictly Stoic, echoed Stoic values in their writings.

The Stoic emphasis on rationality, self-control, and the universality of human reason resonated deeply with Enlightenment thinkers.

20th Century: Stoicism in Pop Culture and Psychology

As the challenges of the modern age became evident in the 20th century, with wars and existential threats, Stoicism offered a way to navigate these turbulent times.

It found its way into popular culture, with figures like James Stockdale, a U.S. Navy vice admiral and prisoner of war, crediting Stoic teachings for his resilience.

Moreover, the latter part of the century saw the rise of cognitive-behavioral therapy (CBT) in psychology, a methodology that drew heavily from Stoic practices. CBT emphasized understanding and changing negative thought patterns, mirroring the Stoic focus on recognizing and challenging irrational beliefs.

21st Century: Modern Stoicism and Self-help

The digital age, with its unique set of challenges, has seen a resurgence in Stoicism, particularly within self-help circles.

Modern Stoicism, with its emphasis on mindfulness, acceptance, and personal responsibility, offers tools to navigate the anxieties of the modern world. Podcasts, blogs, books, personal success stories, and famous personalities have spread awareness, igniting a renewed interest in Stoic practices.

Conclusion

From its humble beginnings on a painted porch in Athens to its profound influence on some of history's greatest minds, Stoicism has left an indelible mark on the philosophical landscape.

Its timeless wisdom, emphasizing inner peace, rationality, and ethical living, continues to find relevance, providing a compass for those seeking guidance in an ever-changing world.

Modern-Day Stoics

In today's fast-paced and often tumultuous world, the ancient philosophy of Stoicism provides a guiding light for many, including many prominent figures whose lives and actions resonate deeply with Stoic principles.

Various individuals embody the principles of ancient Stoicism, offering profound lessons through their journeys. This chapter highlights sixteen contemporary figures who exemplify Stoic virtues in action.

Their stories are a testament to the timeless nature of Stoic wisdom and a source of inspiration, demonstrating how these principles can be harnessed for resilience, purpose, and serenity in today's world.

1. Warren Buffett: Known for his frugality and value investing, Buffett's life reflects Stoic temperance. He avoids excess and practices emotional control, particularly in his investment strategies, demonstrating clear parallels to the Stoic teaching of managing desires and exercising rational judgment.

2. Bill Gates: Gates' philanthropic ventures, particularly his significant contributions to global health and education through the Bill & Melinda Gates Foundation, reflect the Stoic principle of duty to others. His commitment to using his wealth for the greater good shows an understanding of the Stoic belief in community and shared humanity.

3. Steve Jobs: Though known for his intense personality, Jobs often demonstrated the Stoic principle of focusing on what one can control. His famous product presentations were less about the products themselves and more about the user's experience and the intersection of technology and liberal arts, highlighting a Stoic-like understanding of life's broader perspective.

4. Vince Lombardi: One of American sports' most iconic figures, Lombardi exemplified Stoic principles through his unwavering discipline and commitment to excellence. He believed firmly in the power of teamwork and unity of purpose, famously asserting, "A few men working closely together, with discipline and a single-minded commitment to excellence, can succeed against all odds." He was a pillar of self-accountability, constantly pushing himself to new heights and leading by example, thereby fostering a culture of honesty and authentic character building within his team.

This deep-seated belief in selfless collaboration and the pursuit of a higher standard reflects the core Stoic values of wisdom, courage, and justice.

He famously said, "The quality of a person's life is in direct proportion to their commitment to excellence," reflecting the Stoic belief in personal responsibility and the pursuit of virtue through action.

His leadership wasn't about individual accolades but about collective effort and mutual respect, reflecting core Stoic values of collaboration and community. He once attributed the Green Bay Packers' success to their profound sense of camaraderie, saying, "They didn't do it for individual glory. They did it because they loved one another."

His ability to remain unemotional and steadfast in the most high-pressure moments in football highlights his commitment to maintaining an even-keel, a key tenet of Stoicism.

5. James Stockdale: An avowed Stoic, Stockdale credited the philosophy with helping him endure seven and a half years as a prisoner of war. His resilience under unthinkable conditions and horrific torture is a testament to the Stoic teachings of endurance, resilience, and finding inner peace despite external circumstances.

6. The teachings of the **Dalai Lama** on compassion, acceptance, and the transient nature of life find parallels in Stoic philosophy. His emphasis on inner peace, especially in the face of external adversities, resonates with the Stoic idea of maintaining one's inner citadel.

7. Nelson Mandela: Mandela's forgiveness and reconciliation efforts after apartheid are profound examples of Stoic magnanimity and justice. His focus on peace over revenge exemplifies the Stoic belief in rationality and virtue over passion.

8. Malala Yousafzai: Stoicism's resilience is evident in Malala's fight for girls' education despite life-threatening opposition. Her activism, undeterred by near-fatal attacks, embodies the Stoic virtues of courage and persistence for a cause.

9. Oprah Winfrey: Through her career, Oprah has demonstrated Stoic principles by focusing on self-improvement, spiritual growth, and the betterment of others. Her public battles with personal trauma and her initiatives to help others overcome adversity echo the Stoic path of inner healing and service to others.

10. Tim Cook: Cook's quiet demeanor and emphasis on privacy, human rights, and environmental responsibility as Apple's CEO show a commitment to Stoic principles like temperance and justice. He seeks a legacy of moral responsibility, aligning with the Stoic duty to contribute to societal welfare.

11. David Goggins: Former Navy SEAL and ultramarathon runner, Goggins' life reflects Stoic endurance. His philosophy, "40% rule," suggests that when you think you're done, you're only 40% through your capabilities, resonating with the Stoic principle of testing one's limits through rigorous discipline.

12. Ingvar Kamprad, the founder of IKEA, was known for his incredibly modest lifestyle. Flying economy, driving an old Volvo, and frequently visiting his own stores to enjoy a budget meal, Kamprad's life was a vivid illustration of the Stoic values of simplicity and humility.

13. Jeremy Grantham: As an investor, Grantham's Stoic traits are evident in his long-term, dispassionate investment strategy, often avoiding the whims of market emotion. He practices clear-headedness and rational decision-making, key Stoic virtues, especially during economic crises. His focus on sustainability and acknowledgment of the transient nature of market success also parallels Stoicism's emphasis on impermanence and the broader view of societal well-being.

Grantham is known for his extraordinary commitment to philanthropy, particularly his pledge to invest $1 billion in efforts to combat the climate crisis. This move isn't just about charity; it's about responsibility — a concept deeply rooted in Stoic philosophy.

Stoicism teaches that we should live in harmony with our community and environment, acting for the greater good and not just individual gain.

Grantham's focus on environmental sustainability represents the Stoic principle of working towards the welfare of humanity as a whole. His investments are aimed at safeguarding the planet for future generations, an act of profound moral and social responsibility. This reflects the Stoic belief in 'oikeiosis,' the sense of affinity and concern for others' well-being and the understanding that all our actions contribute to a larger social and environmental ecosystem. By taking this bold step, Grantham embodies the Stoic ideals of justice and wisdom, recognizing the interconnectedness of our world and actively working to preserve it.

14. Keanu Reeves: Known for his humility, generosity, and privately dealing with personal tragedies, Reeves' life demonstrates Stoic principles of humility, acceptance, and focusing on actions over words. His low-key lifestyle, despite his fame, aligns with Stoic ideas about the unimportance of material wealth and social status.

15. Chuck Feeney, co-founder of the Duty-Free Shoppers Group, is another embodiment of Stoic generosity. Having given away his multi-billion-dollar fortune to charitable causes, Feeney's commitment to making a difference and living a low-profile life aligns perfectly with Stoic principles of benevolence and living for a purpose greater than oneself.

16. Aung San Suu Kyi: Her long years of house arrest tested her resilience, during which she turned to meditation and reflection, practices akin to Stoic self-dialogue and discipline. Despite her controversial political journey, her early stoicism was evident in her calm demeanor and acceptance of her situation, embodying the Stoic principle of understanding what is within one's control and what is not, and maintaining composure and peace of mind amidst adversity.

These individuals, each in their unique way, showcase how Stoic principles manifest in modern life, emphasizing virtue, endurance, and the greater good. Their lives and decisions reflect Stoicism's enduring relevance and its deep impact on life and the world.

PART II

Stoic Values & Principles

A re you seeking a life of genuine happiness and fulfillment? True and enduring inner peace resides in comprehending the fundamental Stoic virtues, the keys to unlocking a life rich with contentment and serenity.

Stoicism isn't just a collection of lofty ideals but a practical guide to living. At its core lie values and principles that have withstood the test of time, serving as a compass for individuals navigating the complexities of life.

This part of the book delves into these foundational tenets, illuminating the path to inner tranquility and a purposeful existence.

Understanding Stoic values and principles is crucial as they equip us with the wisdom to make conscientious decisions, anchoring us in authenticity and virtue.

These timeless guidelines instill resilience, allowing us to weather life's adversities with grace and poise.

By internalizing these core ideals, we foster a life not just of superficial happiness, but of deep, unwavering contentment regardless of external circumstances.

They become our steady hand in turbulent times, a source of courage and clarity amid confusion, ensuring we live not just reactively, but with purpose and deliberation.

The 4 Cardinal Virtues

At the core of Stoic philosophy lie the four cardinal virtues. These virtues form the basis of moral life in Stoicism and are the foundation of living in harmony with nature.

Wisdom (Practical Wisdom or Prudence)

Wisdom in Stoicism isn't just about acquiring knowledge; it's about applying that knowledge in everyday life. It's the ability to navigate complex situations thoughtfully, make sound decisions, and choose the right actions based on reason.

Everyday Example: Consider you're dealing with overwhelming tasks at work. Instead of succumbing to stress, you employ Stoic wisdom to discern what's within your control. You prioritize tasks, delegate where possible, and understand that doing your best doesn't mean working yourself to exhaustion.

Challenging Situation: If someone betrays your trust, instead of reacting impulsively, you take a step back and reflect on the situation from a rational standpoint. Wisdom allows you to understand human imperfection, manage your emotions, and perhaps give them space to explain, promoting communication over conflict.

Courage (Moral Courage)

Stoic courage isn't recklessness but the resolve to stand firm in the face of challenges. It's about facing daily life's difficulties and moral dilemmas with integrity without compromising on your values for comfort or convenience.

Everyday Example: Moral courage is when, upon witnessing discriminatory behavior, you choose to speak out against it, despite the crowd remaining silent. You're guided not by fear of social ostracism, but by a commitment to justice.

Challenging Situation: If you're faced with a serious health diagnosis, courage is the ability to accept the reality without denial. It involves bravely undergoing necessary treatments, preparing for potential outcomes, and still finding ways to appreciate life's beauties, rather than succumbing to despair.

Justice (Fairness)

Justice involves dealing with others fairly and with kindness, acknowledging our role in society, and contributing to communal well-being. It's about ensuring others' rights are respected as much as our own.

Everyday Example: If you're in a position of power, justice means you make decisions that consider everyone's well-being, not just favoring the elite. It's about creating opportunities for all, treating employees with respect, and giving credit where it's due.

Challenging Situation: Should you come across someone in need — be it a homeless individual or someone requiring assistance — justice compels you to help within your capacity, not turning a blind eye. If you find someone being treated unfairly, you advocate for them, recognizing the injustice they face as detrimental to societal harmony.

Moderation (Self-Control)

Moderation is the ability to regulate one's behaviors and emotions, restraining indulgence in physical and emotional excesses. It's about finding the right balance and not being a slave to one's desires.

Everyday Example: You practice moderation by having a healthy lifestyle, not overindulging in food, or under-indulging either. It's not about severe restrictions but maintaining a balance where you enjoy life without excess.

Challenging Situation: When you're faced with aggressive behavior, perhaps during a heated argument, moderation is what helps you maintain your composure. You listen, respond respectfully, and don't allow your emotions to escalate the situation. It's also the restraint to avoid harmful coping mechanisms, like excessive drinking during stressful times.

These cardinal virtues are interdependent, contributing to a life of eudaimonia, a state of having a good indwelling spirit or being in a contented, happy state of being healthy, purposeful, and fulfilled. Nurturing these virtues requires constant practice and mindfulness, but they promise a life of peace, resilience, and deep contentment, regardless of external circumstances. By understanding and integrating these virtues into daily life, one learns to navigate life's complexities with grace, integrity, and serenity.

The 3 Disciplines

Stoicism is anchored in the practice of consistent disciplines that help individuals navigate the complexities of life.

These disciplines aren't merely theoretical concepts but practical guides that, when applied, can lead to profound personal growth producing enduring tranquility.

Below we delve into the core of Stoic philosophy: the three main disciplines, each one addressing a fundamental aspect of human experience.

The Discipline of Desire (Hormê)

The Discipline of Desire, also known as "the discipline of will," involves our capacity to wish for things correctly. A common source of human misery is the desire for things beyond our control. Stoics understand that this sets us up for disappointment, anxiety, and discontent. Therefore, this discipline focuses on learning to wish things to happen as they do, and only desiring things within one's control.

Practicing this discipline means aligning our desires with reality, embracing fate, and the natural order of the universe. It is about wanting what you have, rather than having what you want.

For instance, rather than desiring wealth, fame, or luxury - external things all outside of our control - we should focus on personal virtues, integrity, and inner peace, which are within our control.

This adjustment in focus frees us from the anxiety of unfulfilled desires and the relentless pursuit of external validations and material possessions.

"Freedom is the only worthy goal in life. It is won by disregarding things that lie beyond our control."

\- Epictetus

The Discipline of Action (Hupexairesis)

The Discipline of Action concerns our social relationships and duties. It is about ensuring our behavior in the world aligns with the Stoic principles of virtue and justice.

This discipline requires that we approach each interaction with mindfulness and intention, contributing to society's betterment and treating others justly, regardless of how they treat us.

This practice involves being mindful of our roles in life — as a family member, a friend, a citizen — and considering what actions we can take to fulfill these roles virtuously.

Whether we're helping a neighbor, being honest in a business transaction, or standing up for what's right, our actions must be guided by reason and the common good, rather than personal gain.

By doing so, we find purpose in contributing to something greater than ourselves and attain fulfillment in knowing that we are living in harmony with our deepest values.

> *"Very little is needed to make a happy life; it is all within yourself, in your way of thinking."*
>
> - Marcus Aurelius

The Discipline of Assent (Sunkatathesis)

The Discipline of Assent revolves around our internal judgments and reactions to external events. It's about exercising critical judgment before agreeing to the impressions we receive from the world.

Stoics believe that things are not upsetting in themselves; it's our judgment of them that upsets us.

Through this discipline, we practice perceiving the world without letting biases or preconceived notions color our perception.

In practice, when we encounter challenges, we pause and assess our initial impressions by asking, "Is this within my control?" If it is, we identify the most virtuous action to take. If it isn't, we practice detachment.

For example, if someone insults us, we might feel inclined to react negatively. However, by utilizing the Discipline of Assent, we would pause, process the insult, and recognize that while we can't control what others say, we can control our reaction, thus preventing anger or resentment.

> *"Better to trip with the feet than with the tongue."*
>
> - Zeno of Citium

These three disciplines work in unison to guide a Stoic through life. They remind us that happiness and tranquility result not from external possessions or accolades but from inner virtue and wisdom.

By mastering our desires, acting with virtue, and assenting only to what is true and good, we forge a life of peace, purpose, and resilience, unswayed by the ever-changing tides of fortune.

The Pathway to a Fulfilling Life

"The happiness of your life depends upon the quality of your thoughts."

- Marcus Aurelius

The ancient school of Stoicism posits more than a philosophy—it's a way of life. Built around ideas of virtue, control, and harmony with nature, its teachings are as applicable today as in ancient times.

Central to Stoicism are several key concepts that guide the pursuit of a good life—a life of eudaimonia. Let's delve into these foundational values and explore their transformative power.

Eudaimonia: The Flourishing Life

At the heart of Stoicism is 'eudaimonia,' often translated as 'happiness' or more accurately as, 'flourishing.' Eudaimonia is the ultimate goal, a state of contentment, peace, and lasting satisfaction achievable through a life of virtue. It isn't about fleeting pleasures or material wealth, but the fulfillment that comes from living in accordance with nature and reason.

By practicing Stoic virtues, individuals can cultivate a resilient character, undisturbed by life's hardships, and find true contentment.

Prosoche: The Art of Mindfulness

'Prosoche' refers to the profound attention we give to our present thoughts and actions. It's about being mindfully present, ensuring that everything we think and do aligns with our rational nature and virtues.

This constant vigilance in daily life, this commitment to intentionality, is crucial in steering away from impulsive reactions and maintaining inner tranquility.

Through prosoche, one guards their rational mind, ensuring each decision is made with clarity and moral purpose.

Pathos: Understanding Destructive Emotions

Stoicism teaches us to transform 'pathos,' the irrational and destructive passions, into constructive feelings.

It doesn't advocate for an emotionless existence but encourages discerning between reflexive emotional impulses and feelings guided by reason.

By understanding the triggers and roots of these destructive passions, we can recalibrate our responses, channeling our energies into actions that contribute to our eudaimonia.

Eupatheiai: Cultivating Positive Emotions

Where pathos are the harmful passions, 'eupatheiai' are their virtuous counterparts—rational feelings that align with our true nature.

These include caution, joy, and wishes, reflecting reasoned responses to circumstances.

Eupatheiai aren't turbulent emotions but serene states, free from internal conflicts. They arise from a sound mind, contributing to a sense of harmony with the world.

Arete: Excellence in Virtue

'Arete,' or virtue, is the cornerstone of Stoic philosophy. It signifies moral excellence and the active practice of virtues like wisdom, courage, justice, and temperance.

Arete isn't a passive quality but a dynamic pursuit of excellence in character, which is reflected in every choice we make.

It's about realizing our highest potential and striving for moral growth, integral to achieving eudaimonia.

"Virtue is nothing else than right reason."

- Seneca

Oikeiosis: Developing Kinship

'Oikeiosis' is the sense of belonging and connectedness with the broader world. It's recognizing ourselves as part of a larger whole and nurturing a sense of care towards others.

This principle guides us to act justly and with kindness, seeing the welfare of others as integral to our own.

Adiaphora: Indifference to Neutrals

'Adiaphora' encompasses things indifferent, neither good nor bad in themselves—like wealth, health, or status.

Stoicism teaches these are not vital for eudaimonia and should neither be sought nor shunned. What matters is how we use them, ensuring they serve virtue.

Our tranquility mustn't rely on externals, but on inner virtue.

In conclusion, the Stoic way of life offers a road map to eudaimonia—a life of genuine fulfillment.

It teaches the cultivation of self-awareness, self-mastery, and sympathy for others, promoting a life in harmony with the world.

By embracing these principles, we can navigate life's complexities with grace, stability, and a sense of purpose, achieving a deep, enduring happiness.

The Stoic Dichotomy: Good, Bad, and Indifferent

"Except for virtue and vice, all else is 'indifferent'."

- Epictetus

Stoicism, a philosophy known for promoting resilience and tranquility, draws clear lines when defining what constitutes a 'good' or 'bad' life. It also offers a unique perspective on the various elements that we often give undue importance to, elements it considers 'indifferent.'

Understanding what Stoicism perceives as good, bad, or indifferent is fundamental to grasping the essence of a Stoic life, particularly when it comes to cultivating happiness and contentment.

The Good: Virtue as the Sole Good

In Stoicism, 'good' is exclusively attributed to what is within us, namely our character and, more precisely, our virtue.

Virtue consists of qualities such as wisdom, courage, justice, and temperance. It is considered the sole good because it is both necessary and sufficient for eudaimonia, a form of profound happiness and fulfillment.

In the Stoic view, a virtuous life is inherently a happy life, regardless of external circumstances.

The Bad: Vice and Moral Corruption

Conversely, 'bad' pertains to the moral failings within us, encompassing traits such as greed, injustice, anger, cowardice, and foolishness.

These vices are reflections of our moral corruption and lead us away from a life of eudaimonia. They represent failures in judgment and character, contributing to an unfulfilled life ruled by passion instead of reason.

"The best answer to anger is silence."

- Marcus Aurelius

The Indifferent: External Circumstances and Possessions

Stoicism categorizes things outside of our moral character as 'indifferents.' These include health, wealth, status, and other external circumstances or possessions.

Indifferents are not inherently bad or good, but their value depends on how they are used. For instance, wealth can be used virtuously to help others or viciously oppress them.

For a Stoic, these external factors are not considered necessary for happiness. They are 'preferred' or 'dispreferred' based on whether they naturally align with our human nature and societal duties. However, they don't affect our ability to live a good life.

Our tranquility and happiness are contingent on our internal state and choices, not our external situation.

The Foundation of Happiness

According to Stoicism, the requirements for a happy life are found within us.

Happiness is achieved through a consistent practice of virtue, maintaining a moral disposition that resonates with our inherent rational nature and social responsibility. It's about responding to life's challenges with wisdom, making decisions with courage, interacting with others justly, and managing desires and fears with temperance.

The pursuit of virtue, the sole good, provides us with freedom from passion-led turmoil and places us in harmony with our true nature and the world. It allows for a serene state of mind, undisturbed by life's adversities and the relentless chase of external validations and material possessions.

In essence, Stoicism's pathway to happiness is grounded in self-control, rationality, and a deep understanding of what we can govern—our judgments, impulses, desires, and aversions.

By focusing on nurturing our inner virtue and regarding externalities as 'indifferent,' we develop resilience, equanimity, and a sense of contentment, irrespective of life's oscillating nature.

By internalizing these Stoic principles, one can embark on a transformative journey towards a life of genuine contentment and peace, unshaken by external circumstances and anchored in moral goodness.

Stoic Principles for Inner Peace & Serenity

These fundamental Stoic concepts can collectively guide you toward a more tranquil and effective life.

The Happiness Triangle

In Stoicism, the pursuit of happiness is a noble one but differs significantly from contemporary understandings of the term.

Stoics believe that happiness results from three core tenets: an accurate understanding of the world (seeing life objectively), an ethical mindset of how to behave (living virtuously), and a clear perception of the things we can control and those we cannot.

This "Happiness Triangle" encourages a life of virtue and wisdom, ensuring that actions and expectations align with life as it is, not as we subjectively perceive it.

Dichotomy of Control

Epictetus introduced an idea that continues to define Stoicism: the Dichotomy of Control.

It asserts that some things are within our control (our actions, thoughts, and feelings), while others are outside it (wealth, health, reputation, and status).

Misery ensues when we mistake external events as being our responsibility or within our power to control.

Understanding this dichotomy liberates us from unnecessary stress. It involves focusing energy on our actions and responses, which are within our control, thus enabling us to let go of unhealthy attachments to outcomes and external circumstances.

By adopting this mindset, individuals can maintain inner peace and clarity, irrespective of life's inherent unpredictability.

Sphere of Influence

The concept of the Sphere of Influence complements the Dichotomy of Control.

While acknowledging that we can't control external events, we recognize our potential influence over circumstances through our reactions to them.

This sphere is where we can exercise some degree of influence, though not absolute control. It involves our relationships, jobs, and social roles.

Operating within our Sphere of Influence requires recognizing our limited power and acting within these constraints with virtue and reason.

For instance, we cannot control a friend's distressing behavior, but we can influence the situation by our response, providing support, or setting boundaries.

Concentric Circles

The theory of Concentric Circles, introduced by Hierocles, expands on our relational duties and affections in the social realm.

At the center is the self, followed by increasing circles of family, local community, country, and finally, humanity.

Stoicism teaches that we should work to draw these circles inward, cultivating a universal affinity and sense of shared fate with all people, promoting a stance of global concern and responsibility.

This practice involves viewing others' welfare as integral to our own – understanding that, as social beings, our well-being is interconnected.

It doesn't diminish personal or familial love but extends compassion and consideration outward, acknowledging the dignity and worth of all individuals.

By understanding these Stoic principles, we learn to navigate life with a grounded sense of what we can change and the wisdom to accept what we cannot.

It teaches us to embrace a global perspective of empathy and interconnectedness.

This framework liberates us from the torment of desire and aversion, guiding us towards a tranquil and contented life, undisturbed by the chaos of external circumstances.

It's about finding serenity within, irrespective of the storm outside, ensuring an untroubled heart and a fortified spirit against life's inevitable adversities.

PART III

Stoic Skills for a Happy Life

Embarking on the path of Stoicism unlocks skills pivotal for nurturing a fulfilling life. This ancient philosophy offers profound wisdom that fosters inner peace, imbues calm, and fortifies the mind against life's incessant upheavals. With these skills, you'll unearth an unshakeable confidence and courage, cultivating inner strength and resilience that act as your armor against fears, negative thoughts, anxiety, and depression. Stoicism lights the way in times of confusion, helping you navigate toward your true path, shielding your heart from disappointment, and healing from grief and loss. Embrace these lessons and discover a life not dictated by external circumstances, but steered by wisdom, serenity, and purposeful joy.

Steadying the Mind

Easy Stoic Strategies for Conquering Negativity, Anxiety, and Depression

Life invariably brings challenges that can stir negative thoughts, fears, and sometimes plunge us into the depths of despair. Stoicism doesn't promise a life without troubles, but it offers potent tools to maintain inner tranquility against life's storms.

Below are meditations, exercises, and pieces of wisdom that can serve as your armor and shield in your battles against negativity, anxiety, and depression.

1. Overcoming Negative Thoughts: The Stoic Pause

Negative thoughts are often automatic, uninvited guests of the mind. Stoicism teaches us to create a mental space—"The Stoic Pause"—before responding to these intrusions.

- *Exercise: Observe, Don't Absorb.* The moment you recognize a negative thought, envision it as an external entity. You're not your thoughts; you're the observer. Analyze this thought as if evaluating someone else's: Is it rational? What evidence contradicts it? This detachment is your mental sanctuary.

- *Meditation: Dichotomy of Control.* Reflect deeply on what is within your control and what isn't. Understand that your thoughts are yours to accept or dismiss. You can't control external events, but you can control your interpretations and reactions.

"You have power over your mind - not outside events. Realize this, and you will find strength."

- Marcus Aurelius

2. Overcoming Fears & Anxiety: Premeditatio Malorum (Negative Visualization)

Anxiety stems from fearing the unknown and feeling helpless.

Stoicism arms us against anxiety with "Premeditatio Malorum," a strategy of anticipating potential issues and preparing to address them.

- *Exercise: What's the Worst That Could Happen?* Regularly, consider the worst-case scenarios in various aspects of your life. Then, plan how you'd respond. This planning transforms the unknown into a game plan, reducing anxiety.

- *Meditation: The Fortress of Tranquility.* Spend quiet moments constructing your mental fortress. Each calming breath builds stronger walls. Each moment of mindfulness adds protective layers, ensuring fears don't breach your peace.

3. Overcoming Depression: The View from Above & Gratitude Meditation

Depression often involves feeling stuck in a painful situation or mindset. Stoicism offers perspectives to lessen this burden and reframe our understanding of our circumstances.

- *Exercise: The View from Above.* Visualize observing yourself from a great height, seeing your life and everyone's as part of a larger whole. This shift in perspective, although it doesn't negate your feelings, can reduce the weight of personal suffering and highlight that you're not alone in your struggles.

- *Meditation: Gratitude and Moment Maximization.* Each day, meditate on what you're thankful for, no matter how small. Reflect on the air filling your lungs, the beauty in nature, or the kindness of a stranger. Recognize these as gifts and maximize even the smallest positive moments, letting them be your torch in dark times.

These Stoic practices aren't just theoretical—they're practical, time-tested mental strategies, refined over centuries to fortify your psychological resilience.

They don't erase life's difficulties, but they can equip you with the mental fortitude to confront your inner demons.

By consistently practicing these exercises, you empower yourself to rise above the internal turbulence of negative thoughts, fears, and depression, finding serenity in any storm.

Illuminating the Path

Stoic Approaches to Thinking Clearly and Acting Decisively

In the tumultuous seas of life, our minds can often become clouded, leading us astray from our chosen path and causing unnecessary distress.

Stoicism, with its profound wisdom, provides practical exercises for cutting through the mental fog, promoting clarity of thought, and guiding purposeful action.

This chapter delves into specific Stoic meditations and exercises designed to illuminate your mind and energize your actions.

1. Discerning the Essential: The Stoic Inner Dialogue

Confusion often arises from an overload of conflicting thoughts and desires. Stoicism introduces the practice of inner dialogue to sift through the cacophony and grasp what truly matters.

- *Exercise: Morning Reflections.* Begin your day with a quiet moment, asking yourself: What is truly important for today? What deserves my energy? Visualize the tasks ahead and distinguish between meaningful goals and distractions. By setting clear intentions, you construct a mental blueprint for a purpose-driven day.

2. Embracing Rational Judgment: The Power of Objective Perception

Our perceptions are frequently colored by personal biases and emotions, a direct path to clouded judgment. Stoicism emphasizes perceiving events as they truly are, free from subjective coloring.

- *Meditation: The Observer's Mind.* Allocate a few moments daily to practice viewing your thoughts and feelings as an impartial observer. This mental step back allows emotional distance, facilitating a more rational response to situations. It's not about negating emotions but giving space to reason in interpreting your experiences.

3. Focused Resolve: The Clarity in Action Exercise

Procrastination and hesitation often stem from unclear objectives and priorities, leading to stagnation and regret. Stoicism promotes decisive action rooted in your values and objectives.

- *Exercise: The Single-Tasking Practice.* In a world that glorifies multitasking, embrace single-tasking. Select a task aligned with your fundamental values and devote your undivided attention to it. This concentration amplifies engagement and performance, turning actions into more meaningful and fulfilling experiences.

4. Evening Wisdom: Reflective Meditation on Actions

Clarity is not only about forecasting or being immersed in the current task but also about learning from what has transpired.

- *Meditation: The Day's Review.* Each evening, reflect on your day's actions. What was done in accordance with your values? What wasn't? Recognize achievements, learn from missteps, and plan for improvements. This reflective practice reinforces clear thinking patterns and fosters personal growth.

Stoicism is not merely a theoretical field of philosophy; it's a practical guide for living a fulfilled life.

Through these daily practices, Stoicism teaches us to clear the mental clutter, focus our energies judiciously, and live each day with deliberate intention.

By continually refining our thoughts and actions, we forge a life of clarity, purpose, and profound contentment.

Shielding the Heart

How to Prevent Disappointment and Heartache

In the unpredictable journey of life, heartache and disappointment are often unwelcome companions.

Stoicism, a philosophy built on the bedrock of resilience and clear understanding of human nature, provides practical wisdom that guards our inner tranquility against such emotional upheavals.

This chapter delves into various Stoic practices designed to arm you against the common vulnerabilities of disappointment and heartache.

1. Premeditation of Adversities: Embracing the Worst-Case Scenario

Stoicism advocates for a proactive approach - envisaging the worst-case scenario, not to induce fear, but to diminish the shock and paralysis that come with unforeseen events.

- *Meditation: The Future Projection.* In a quiet space, close your eyes and visualize a situation unfolding not as you hope, but in the most challenging way possible. Feel the emotions, analyze your reactions, and mentally rehearse your responses. This form of visualization strengthens emotional preparedness and resilience.

2. Voluntary Discomfort: The Art of Going Without

Sometimes, the depth of our attachment only becomes apparent in absence. Stoics practice intentional self-denial to appreciate and understand the real value of their comforts.

- *Exercise: The Path of Intentional Loss.* Choose something you enjoy or rely on daily. It could be a luxury, such as your smartphone, favorite food, or even the convenience of a car. Go without it for a set period. The initial discomfort is an enlightening journey towards realizing you can indeed live happily without much of what you believe is essential.

3. The Discipline of Assent: Releasing Attachments

Understanding the true nature and value of things is crucial in Stoicism. It helps in releasing our misguided attachments, leading to unrealistic expectations and subsequent disappointments.

- *Meditation: The Nature of Things.* Meditate on the impermanent, borrowed nature of everything you own and everyone you know. Reflect on how attachments often contribute more to your distress than the actual value of the object or person. This meditation helps in letting go and finding peace in simplicity and the moment.

4. Dichotomy of Control: Navigating through Disappointments

Recognizing what is within our control helps prevent disappointment. It's the understanding that our efforts are within our power, but the outcomes are not always.

- *Exercise: The Sphere of Influence.* On a piece of paper, create two columns. List what's within your control (your actions, efforts, thoughts) and what's not (others' feelings, actions, world events). Regularly remind yourself to release the emotional burden tied to what you cannot control.

5. Practicing Gratitude: The Antidote to Heartache

In the midst of trials, gratitude stands as a powerful force that redirects focus from what is lacking or lost to what is present and valuable.

- *Activity: The Gratitude Journal.* Dedicate time each day to write down three things you're grateful for, no matter how small. Over time, this practice cultivates a sustained sense of contentment, resilience against disappointment, and a profound appreciation for life's blessings, shielding you from persistent heartache.

By integrating these exercises into your daily routine, you gradually equip yourself with the wisdom to prevent disappointments and the resilience to handle heartache.

These practices aren't about escaping reality but fortifying your inner self to face life's vicissitudes with a steadfast spirit.

Stoicism teaches that preventing disappointment and heartache begins with internal work, reshaping our perspectives, responses, and understanding of life's intricate tapestry.

Overcoming Grief & Loss

Navigating the Storms

Loss and grief are among life's most challenging storms.

Stoicism doesn't offer a way around these human experiences but provides a compass to navigate through them with grace and resilience. It teaches acceptance of life's impermanence and helps cultivate a profound understanding that what we lose was never truly ours, but rather something entrusted to us for a time.

Below are Stoic teachings, exercises, and meditations to anchor your soul in times of loss and grief.

1. Understanding Impermanence: The Philosophy of Transience

Everything is in flux. Understanding and accepting the transient nature of life is foundational in Stoicism, helping us cope with loss.

- *Meditation: Contemplating the Cycles.* Dedicate time to meditate on nature's cycles, observing how seasons change, flowers bloom and wither, and stars burn out. Recognize that change and loss are natural and inevitable, which brings a certain peace in knowing you are part of this grand cosmic dance.

2. 'It Was Returned': The Borrowed Nature of Existence

Stoicism gently reminds us that everything we "lose" was merely returned. Our loved ones, possessions, and even our lives are temporary gifts.

- *Exercise: The Practice of 'Praemeditatio Malorum' (Negative Visualization).* In quiet reflection, consider the potential loss of someone or something dear to you, understanding it as part of life's contract. This practice, far from morbid, helps in appreciating what you have and softening the blow when loss occurs.

3. Harnessing Rationality: Separating Pain from Suffering

Pain is inevitable; suffering is optional. Stoicism teaches that our judgments about loss contribute more to our suffering than the loss itself.

- *Exercise: The Dichotomy of Control in Grief.* Write down your feelings and identify which aspects of the situation are within your control and which aren't. This distinction is crucial in focusing your energy effectively during challenging times and avoiding the anguish of attempting to change what cannot be changed.

4. The Healing Power of Service: Redirecting Focus through Altruism

One of the most therapeutic exercises in the face of loss is shifting focus from oneself and serving others.

- *Activity: The Gift of Giving.* Engage in acts of kindness, volunteer, or help someone in need. Service helps in regaining a sense of purpose, creating a positive impact, and is a reminder that you can still contribute to the world in meaningful ways, despite your loss.

5. Journaling through Grief: The Stoic's Chronicle

Expressive writing can be a powerful healing tool, providing a space to express emotions, reflect on them, and make sense of your journey.

- *Exercise: The Reflective Ledger.* Keep a regular journal. Write about your memories, express gratitude for the time spent with lost loved ones or for what past opportunities taught you. Make sure to acknowledge your emotions and milestones in the healing process.

Stoicism's serene wisdom doesn't make grief painless. Instead, it offers a perspective that makes the burden more bearable, reminding us that we are participants in a larger order of things where loss is natural.

In embracing these practices, we find the strength to continue, the resilience to grow, and the clarity to appreciate the preciousness of the present moment.

Through Stoicism, we learn that even in the depth of loss, there lies a path leading back to peace and wholeness.

"When jarred, unavoidably, by circumstances, revert at once to yourself, and don't lose the rhythm more than you can help. You'll have a better grasp of harmony if you keep going back to it."

- Marcus Aurelius

PART IV

Practical Stoic Meditations & Exercises

To help us create a good life marked by tranquility, courage, and wisdom, Stoicism provides practical exercises that ground us in the present and free us from the shackles of our ordinary disturbances.

In essence, these Stoic practices are tools designed to set you free from the fears, anxieties, and false beliefs that disturb your mind. They guide you towards a peaceful existence, where happiness emanates from your very being, unaffected by the changing tides of life.

Each exercise, though simple, is a step towards profound internal stability and serene understanding of the world within and around you.

1. Amor Fati

Embrace Everything Life Throws Your Way

Amor Fati, or "love of fate," is about more than mere acceptance; it's about loving whatever happens. It's the belief that all experiences, positive or negative, are necessary for your growth.

Exercise: Daily Reflection for Unconditional Embrace

Each evening, reflect on your day's events, including challenges. Consider how they shaped you, how you responded, and write down why you're better because of them. This habit helps reframe potentially negative experiences as beneficial for your personal journey.

This practice contributes to happiness by removing the burden of bitterness toward life's unavoidable challenges. It builds resilience, ensuring confidence and inner peace, knowing that you're growing and improving every day.

2. Memento Mori

Make the Most Out of Your Life

"Memento Mori," or remember that you will die, serves as a grounding mechanism, emphasizing the transience of life.

Exercise: The Mirror of Mortality

Each morning, take a moment to look into the mirror and remind yourself that life is fleeting. This acknowledgment isn't meant to be morbid; instead, it's there to inspire you to live your life fully and with integrity, free of trivial fears and anxieties.

By regularly reminding yourself of your own mortality, you learn to value your time and focus on what truly matters, fostering genuine happiness and peace that isn't rattled by everyday inconveniences.

"He who fears death will never do anything worthy of a man who is alive."

- Seneca

3. Negative Visualization

Resilience against Life's Challenges

Negative Visualization involves routinely considering worst-case scenarios. This practice serves not to induce fear but to acknowledge that difficulties may arise, preparing us emotionally and mentally.

Exercise: Preparing for the Storm

Set aside a few minutes each day to consider the potential loss of what you treasure. Visualize life without certain comforts, or even loved ones. It's a stark practice but serves to highlight your blessings and reduce any undue attachments.

This exercise is liberating. By confronting your fears, you dismantle their power. Anticipating challenges reduces anxiety, as you've already lived through these scenarios in your mind. It allows you to appreciate what you have, fostering happiness, and instills a calm preparedness for the future.

"We suffer more often in imagination than in reality."

- Seneca

4. A View from Above

Gaining Perspective on Life's Events

The practice of "A View from Above" helps individuals transcend the immediacy of their circumstances, offering a broader perspective on life's events.

Exercise: Cosmic Contemplation

Find a quiet space and close your eyes. Visualize yourself from above, first from the ceiling, then the rooftop, and further upward until you're viewing Earth from space. See your issues and life events as part of a larger whole. Recognize the vastness of existence and ponder your place within the cosmos.

This meditation instills a sense of humility, reducing the magnitude of personal problems and encouraging a more tranquil response to life's challenges. The recognition of our smallness in the grand scheme of things can be profoundly liberating and stress-relieving.

5. Universal Perspective

Understanding Our Place in the Whole

Stoicism teaches that we are part of a larger universal whole. The practice of Universal Perspective involves seeing ourselves within the context of everything that exists.

Exercise: Reflection on Universal Community

In a relaxed position, reflect on the interconnectedness of all things. Think about the air shared between all beings, the vast expanse of history and the future. Acknowledge your role in this larger existence, respecting its beauty and complexity.

By acknowledging our role in the larger tapestry of existence, we become more patient and understanding. It helps diminish the ego, alleviating conflict rooted in personal entitlement and fostering a deep, enduring sense of peace.

6. Being Present & Grounded

The Antidote to Anxiety & Regret

The exercise of Being Present and Grounded is an antidote to the sprawling anxieties about the future or regrets about the past.

Exercise: The Anchor of Sensation

Focus on your senses in the moment. What do you hear, feel, or smell? Anchor yourself in the physical experience of now. When your mind wanders to past or future events, gently bring your focus back to your immediate sensory experiences.

This practice is instrumental in reducing anxieties and regrets that don't serve our present moment. It encourages a form of active mindfulness that can make us more focused, productive, and calm, accepting the only reality - the present.

"Reject your sense of injury, and the injury itself disappears."
- Marcus Aurelius

7. Circling the Present

Embracing the Here and Now

Circling the Present is about continuously bringing our focus back to the present moment, where our power truly lies.

Exercise: Circle of Awareness - Draw a small circle around yourself. This is your space of influence, your present moment. Whenever your mind starts to wander into territories of 'what-ifs' or 'should-haves,' visualize bringing those thoughts back into your circle, grounding them in the reality of the moment.

Actively practicing this brings a form of mental clarity, aiding in decision-making based on present facts, not uncertain futures or unchangeable pasts. It's a reminder of the serenity found in accepting our current situation and recognizing that this moment is our most significant opportunity.

8. Reserve Clause

Navigating Uncertainty with Wisdom

The "Reserve Clause" in Stoicism is a powerful reminder to maintain a form of mental reservation when planning or expecting outcomes, acknowledging that the result is ultimately beyond our complete control.

Exercise: Conditional Commitment

When you set goals or make plans, mentally add the phrase "Fate permitting" or "If nothing prevents me." This mental note is not to make an excuse for not reaching the goal but to remind yourself of the realities outside your control.

Embracing the Reserve Clause helps in mitigating disappointment, as it mentally prepares you for any outcome, ensuring that unforeseen changes don't disrupt your inner peace. It promotes a proactive form of humility, understanding that our efforts are part of the equation, not the entire sum.

9. True Meaning of Success

Redefining Achievement

Stoicism invites us to redefine success, suggesting that the true victory lies in performing our roles well, irrespective of the outcome. It's the pursuit that counts, not always the attainment.

Exercise: The Journal of Effort

At the end of each day, write down the efforts you made towards your goals, focusing less on whether they were achieved. Celebrate the quality and intention of your work, recognizing these efforts as successes in themselves.

This practice cultivates happiness that doesn't hinge on outcomes. It encourages a sense of satisfaction and pride in the work itself, fostering a more stable and enduring form of contentment. This understanding of success forms a sturdy shield against the unpredictability of life.

10. Hope & Fear

Balancing Aspirations with Reality

Stoicism teaches us to temper our hopes and fears by facing reality as it is, not as we wish it to be. By managing these emotions, we remain anchored in the present.

Exercise: Reflections on Reality

Consider your current hopes and fears, then objectively identify what aspects are within your control. For those elements outside your control, prepare mentally for any outcome, understanding that external factors do not define your inner worth or peace.

This balancing act between hope and fear prevents us from becoming overconfident or paralyzed by fear. It fosters a resilient spirit that can remain hopeful yet realistic, courageous yet prudent.

11. Gratitude

Embracing Life as It Is

A cornerstone of Stoic joy. We cultivate contentment by appreciating what we have rather than lamenting what we don't.

Exercise: Daily Gratitude Reflection

Identify three things you are grateful for each day, big or small. Regularly remind yourself to love what you already have - from personal attributes and relationships to simple daily occurrences.

The practice of gratitude is transformative. It shifts your focus from lack to abundance, from missed opportunities to the plethora of blessings that fill your life. This simple shift in perspective is powerful enough to lift the spirit even in times of hardship, fostering lasting happiness and peace.

These Stoic principles and exercises continue the journey toward understanding and embracing the ebb and flow of life. They remind us that our power lies in effort and attitude, not in the whims of external circumstances. By accepting this, we unlock a level of enduring tranquility, unshaken by the tides of fortune and misfortune alike.

The next exercises address key practices that focus on liberating oneself from the often unacknowledged chains of desire and fear that tether us to unrest.

12. The Path to Inner Peace

Freeing Yourself from Attachments

Attachments, especially those material in nature, often serve as silent tyrants over our peace of mind. Stoicism teaches us to free ourselves from the overbearing weight of these attachments.

Exercise: Detachment Assessment

Make a list of items you believe you couldn't live without. One by one, imagine you have lost each of these items, and reflect on why life would and should continue. Understanding and embracing the impermanent nature of all things helps in cultivating a mind unshackled by loss.

This practice isn't about fostering a negative outlook but about nurturing a form of liberating resilience. It leads to the understanding that our spirit, our true essence, doesn't rely on external attachments for peace, thereby establishing a steady, untroubled mind.

13. Releasing the Fear of Loss and Lack

A preoccupation with loss and scarcity can lead to a life experienced as a continuous, unsettling chase. Stoicism offers a perspective shift.

Exercise: Contemplation of Impermanence - Regularly take a moment to reflect on the transient nature of all things—jobs, relationships, life itself. This contemplation can help in gradually releasing the deep-seated fear of loss and the anxiety that accompanies this fear.

Acknowledging and accepting impermanence fosters a form of mental and emotional release from the anxieties of future uncertainties, grounding you in the present.

14. The True Riches

Simplicity and Less

Stoicism advocates for a simple life where true wealth is found in virtues and experiences rather than material abundance.

Exercise: The Minimalist Approach - Periodically assess your belongings and lifestyle. Identify what isn't essential and consider simplifying areas of material excess. This practice isn't about deprivation but about identifying what genuinely contributes to your happiness and peace of mind.

Embracing simplicity helps in recognizing that the chase for more often leads to an unquenchable thirst. A life of less is not only more sustainable but often more fulfilling, as it shifts the focus from quantity to quality, from chaos to peace.

15. Embracing Discomfort

Finding Peace & Happiness through Voluntary Suffering

The practice of voluntary suffering—choosing to forego comfort—prepares us for life's inevitable hardships, making us appreciate what we have and strengthening us against what we fear.

Exercise: Deliberate Discomfort - Once in a while, engage in an activity that's challenging or slightly uncomfortable, such as fasting, cold showers, or sleeping on the floor. This doesn't just build tolerance for different levels of hardship but also provides a deeper appreciation for your usual comforts.

Voluntary suffering in moderation can significantly diminish the fear of loss and hardship by familiarizing yourself with discomfort. It's a reminder that you can endure, adapt, and thrive, which contributes profoundly to inner peace and confidence.

> *"The universe is change; our life is what our thoughts make it."*
>
> - Marcus Aurelius

These practices serve as reminders that the pursuit of external abundance often leads to an inner vacuum of chronic dissatisfaction and unrest. Conversely, the path of intentional simplicity, acceptance of life's ebbs and flows, and the deliberate embrace of discomfort fortifies our internal fortress, equipping us with the strength, contentment, and tranquility necessary to navigate life's tumultuous waters.

Stoicism in Everyday Life

"Difficulties strengthen the mind, as labor does the body."

- Seneca

Life is a complex mosaic of experiences, responsibilities, and emotions. Amidst this, maintaining equilibrium is a challenge.

Stoicism endows us with practical tools to navigate various aspects of our lives, encouraging a happier, more content existence.

Here's how Stoic principles can be seamlessly integrated into different facets of everyday life.

1. Success & Purpose: Defining True Achievement

Stoicism redefines 'success' not as a material condition but as living in harmony with nature, which includes our own true self and purpose. It's about aligning with our inner virtues rather than external validations.

- *Daily Reflection:* Evaluate your day based on virtue and moral purpose rather than material gains. Did your actions align with your core values? How can you make better choices tomorrow?

2. Business & Career: Stoic Resilience in Professional Endeavors

In the professional realm, Stoicism advises focusing on effort over outcome. It teaches resilience, ethical conduct, and decision-making free from emotional bias, crucial for career growth and business management.

- *The Sphere of Control:* List out aspects under your control (work ethic, effort, integrity) and things not (market trends, opinions). Focus your energy only where it counts and detach emotionally from the rest.

3. Family: Building Strong, Virtuous Bonds

For a Stoic, family is not just an emotional haven but also a place to practice virtues like patience, understanding, and love. It's about leading by example and nurturing relationships through active presence and unconditional support.

- *Mindful Interactions:* Practice active listening in conversations with family members, acknowledging feelings without judgment. It strengthens bonds, ensuring a supportive, loving environment.

4. Harmonious Relationships: Cultivating Understanding and Empathy

Stoicism promotes harmony in relationships through empathy, open communication, and understanding, asserting that we're part of a larger community and our actions impact others.

- *The Daily Audit:* Reflect on your interactions at day's end. Were they in line with the Stoic virtues of kindness, honesty, and respect? How can you improve?

5. Social Life: Engaging with the Community

Stoicism encourages playing an active, positive role in society, contributing to the well-being of others while cultivating self-contentment. It's about balancing social obligations with personal peace.

- *Voluntary Contributions:* Engage in voluntary social work. Helping others provides a sense of purpose and happiness, resonating with the Stoic principle of mutual welfare.

6. Health Challenges: Stoic Strength in Adversity

Health crises test our spirit and resilience. Stoicism teaches acceptance of what we can't change while exerting control over our attitudes and responses.

- *Contemplative Acceptance:* In quiet reflection, acknowledge your health status and circumstances beyond your control. Focus on your response, finding strength in adversity, and appreciate life in its current form.

Incorporating Stoicism into everyday life doesn't demand drastic changes but rather a shift in perspective—seeing trials as opportunities for growth, valuing virtue over material success, and cherishing serenity over chaos.

By practicing these small, daily exercises rooted in Stoic philosophy, we can profoundly enhance our internal peace, happiness, and overall life satisfaction.

In this endeavor, Stoicism serves as a guiding light, helping us find contentment and joy in both tumultuous storms and peaceful harbors of life.

PART V

90-Day Stoic Journal

DAY 1: THE REALM OF CONTROL

DAY 2: CALM AMIDST CHAOS

DAY 3: LIFE UNCLUTTERED

DAY 4: EMBRACING IMPERMANENCE

DAY 5: LIBERATION FROM ATTACHMENTS

DAY 6: LIFE'S FLEETING NATURE

DAY 7: CHALLENGE YOUR ASSUMPTIONS

DAY 8: COURAGE IN REFLECTION

DAY 9: CONFIDENCE VS. PRIDE

DAY 10: BEYOND FAMILIAR BOUNDS

DAY 11: ACCEPT CRITIQUE

DAY 1:

THE REALM OF

CONTROL

"Some things are in our control and others not."

- Epictetus, Enchiridion, 1.1

Clearly recognizing what we can influence and what we cannot is crucial for our mental well-being.

Meditation: Reflect on situations where you felt out of control. Were those things truly within your power to change?

DAY 2:
CALM AMIDST
CHAOS

"At the center of the storm, there is calm."

- Seneca, Letters, 71.14

Seneca reminds us that inner peace is attainable, even in the midst of dark and scary turmoil.

Meditation: Recall a moment you remained tranquil amidst chaos. How did that serenity influence your perspective and actions?

DAY 3:
LIFE UNCLUTTERED

"Wealth consists not in having great possessions, but in having few wants."

- Epictetus, Enchiridion, 1.2

Epictetus teaches that true riches lie in simplicity and contentment.

Meditation: Imagine a day without excess.

What unnecessary things or desires can you let go of to embrace a more fulfilled, meaningful, and virtuous life?

_____

_____

_____

_____

_____

DAY 4:

EMBRACING

IMPERMANENCE

"Loss is nothing else but change,
and change is nature's delight."
- Marcus Aurelius, Meditations, 7.18

Aurelius suggests that change, even loss, is a natural process to be embraced.

Meditation: Visualize life without a prized possession.

How does this visualization help you appreciate its presence, foster gratitude for what you do have right now, and prepare for its potential absence?

_____

_____

_____

DAY 5:

LIBERATION FROM

ATTACHMENTS

"Attach yourself to what is spiritually superior, regardless of what other people think or do."

- Seneca, Letters, 8.5

Seneca advises anchoring oneself in virtues rather than external validations.

Meditation: Reflect on a time you clung to something or someone.

How can you shift your focus to inner values to free yourself from such attachments?

DAY 6:

LIFE'S FLEETING

NATURE

"Death smiles at us all,
but all a man can do is smile back."
- Marcus Aurelius, Meditations, 2.11

Marcus Aurelius underscores life's transience and encourages us to embrace its ephemerality.

Meditation: Ponder your mortality.

How does this reflection intensify your gratitude for the present and urge you to seize each day?

_____

_____

_____

_____

DAY 7:
CHALLENGE YOUR
ASSUMPTIONS

"First say to yourself what you would be; and then do what you have to do."

- Epictetus, Enchiridion, 1.3

Epictetus prompts us to align actions with conscious decisions, not just assumptions.

Meditation: Recall a time you acted on assumption not on logic.

How can you ensure your actions stem from reflection rather than unchallenged beliefs?

_____

_____

_____

_____

DAY 8: COURAGE IN REFLECTION

"It is not because things are difficult that we do not dare; it is because we do not dare that they are difficult."

- Seneca, Letters, 22.5

Seneca emphasizes the power of courage over adversity.

Meditation: Remember a moment you exhibited bravery. How did confronting fear then shape your understanding of what you're truly capable of now?

_____

_____

_____

_____

_____

DAY 9: CONFIDENCE VS. PRIDE

"Arrogance is the obstruction of wisdom."

- Epictetus, Discourses, 2.17.33

Epictetus warns that overconfidence blinds us to learning and growth.

Meditation: Reflect on an instance where you felt confident. Was it genuine self-assurance or veiled arrogance?

How can you nurture true confidence?

DAY 10:

BEYOND FAMILIAR BOUNDS

"Life begins at the end of your comfort zone."

- Seneca, Letters, 76.4

Seneca encourages us to embrace discomfort as a catalyst for growth.

Meditation: Consider a time you remained within your comfort boundaries. What might you discover by daring to venture beyond? How can you push your limits today?

_____

_____

_____

_____

DAY 11:

ACCEPT CRITIQUE

"It is the mark of an educated mind to be able to entertain a thought without accepting it."

- Marcus Aurelius, Meditations, 4.22

Marcus Aurelius highlights the value of discernment when faced with critique.

Meditation: Imagine receiving criticism. How can you respond with grace, taking what is constructive and discarding what isn't, while maintaining your equanimity?

_____

_____

_____

_____

_____

DAY 12:

EMBRACING THE

EBB AND FLOW

"Every setback is a setup for a comeback."

- Seneca, Letters, 71.12

Seneca reminds us that in the grand scheme, setbacks are but temporary pauses, not an end.

Meditation: Reflect on a perceived failure. How did it pave the way for growth or a new beginning? How can you reframe challenges as opportunities for resilience?

_____

_____

_____

_____

_____

DAY 13:
MISTAKES AS
MILESTONES

"From every wound, there is a scar, and every scar tells a story. A story that says, 'I survived.'"

- Marcus Aurelius, Meditations, 6.30

Aurelius emphasizes the transformative power of our past errors.

Meditation: Recall a past mistake. How did it shape your wisdom and character? What lessons did you glean from that experience?

_____

_____

_____

_____

_____

DAY 14:

HUMILITY IN

FEEDBACK

"It's not what you say out of your mouth that determines your life; it's what you whisper to yourself that has the most power."

- Epictetus, Enchiridion, 3.22

Epictetus stresses the importance of self-awareness and the value of external perspectives.

Meditation: When was the last time you sought honest feedback? How can you embrace it as a tool for growth and humility?

_____

_____

_____

_____

DAY 15: CULTIVATING GRATITUDE

"True happiness is to enjoy the present, without anxious dependence upon the future."

- Seneca, Letters, 16.7

Seneca speaks of the joy rooted in appreciating the present moment.

Meditation: Consider your current blessings. What three things are you profoundly thankful for today?

_____

_____

_____

_____

_____

DAY 16: SAVORING SIMPLICITY

"It is not the man who has too little, but the man who craves more, that is poor."

- Seneca, Letters, 2.6

Seneca celebrates contentment in life's modest offerings over the pursuit of excess.

Meditation: Ponder the simple pleasures and small joys you've recently experienced. What little everyday experiences or simple things bring you contentment?

DAY 17:
BLESSINGS IN
DISGUISE

"Difficulties strengthen the mind, as labor does the body."

— Seneca, Letters, 36.1

Seneca underscores the transformative power of challenges in refining our character.

Meditation: Recall a hardship you faced. What unexpected blessings or lessons emerged from that ordeal?

How has adversity, in retrospect, shaped a better path for you?

_____

_____

_____

_____

DAY 18:
EMBRACING THE
NOW

"Do not spoil what you have by desiring what you have not; remember that what you now have was once among the things you only hoped for."

- Epictetus, Enchiridion, 1.4

Epictetus emphasizes the beauty of living in and appreciating the present.

Meditation: Reflect on today. How can you find joy in this very moment?

_____

_____

_____

_____

DAY 19:
CONTENTMENT

"Complaining does not work as a strategy. We all have finite time and energy. Any time we spend whining is unlikely to help us achieve our goals."

- Marcus Aurelius, Meditations, 7.28

Aurelius encourages proactive action over passive lamenting.

Meditation: Imagine a day free from grievances. How does it change your interactions and inner peace?

What steps can you take to reduce unnecessary complaints in your daily life?

_____

_____

_____

_____

_____

DAY 20:

REFRAMING INNER

DIALOGUE

"The greater the difficulty,
the more the glory in surmounting it."

— Epictetus, Enchiridion, 1.10

Epictetus reminds us to turn challenges, even internal ones, into opportunities for growth.

Meditation: Reflect on a recent instance of negative self-talk. How can you challenge and transform those thoughts into constructive ones to empower your actions and beliefs?

_____

_____

_____

_____

DAY 21:

EMBRACING YOUR

JOURNEY

"Compare yourself only with yourself."

- Seneca, Letters, 44.10

Seneca emphasizes the value of personal growth over societal measures of success.

Meditation: Think of a time you measured your worth against someone else's. How can you redirect that energy to appreciate your unique path and growth to uplift your spirit and self-worth?

_____

_____

_____

_____

_____

DAY 22:

THE MEANING OF VIRTUE

"Virtue is nothing else than right reason."

- Seneca, Letters, 71.13

Seneca defines virtue as our ability to act with wisdom and integrity.

Meditation: Ponder the virtues that resonate most with you. How do you embody them in your daily life?

_____

_____

_____

_____

_____

DAY 23:
STANDING FIRM IN
VALUES

---

*"Let your every deed and word and thought be those of one
who could depart from life this moment."*

- Marcus Aurelius

Aurelius speaks of the importance of acting in alignment with
one's core beliefs.

Meditation: Reflect on an instance where you stood by your
principles. How did it shape the outcome and your perception of
self-worth?

DAY 24:

COURAGE IN TRUTH

"A liar needs a good memory."

- Seneca, Letters, 88.5

Seneca highlights the simplicity and strength found in truthfulness.

Meditation: Think of a time when honesty was challenging.

How did you navigate the situation?

What lessons did it offer about the power of truth, even when faced with adversity or discomfort?

_____

_____

_____

_____

_____

DAY 25:

LIVING INTEGRITY

"Just that you do the right thing.
The rest doesn't matter."

- Marcus Aurelius, Meditations, 9.20

Aurelius underscores the paramount importance of integrity in all actions, big or small.

Meditation: Imagine living with unwavering integrity. How do your interactions and choices differ?

How can you infuse more authenticity and honor in your life?

DAY 26:

VIRTUE'S REWARD

"Virtue is its own reward."

- Seneca, Letters, 81.19

Seneca conveys that the true value of virtue lies not in external accolades but in the internal fulfillment it brings.

Meditation: Reflect on an act of virtue you've performed without expecting anything in return. How did you feel?

How can embracing virtue enrich your life's journey?

DAY 27:

NAVIGATING MORAL

CROSSROADS

"Difficult choices, unlike red wine, rarely improve with age."
- Seneca, Letters, 58.4

Seneca emphasizes the importance of thoughtful decision making based on virtue.

Meditation: Consider a recent or potential moral dilemma. How would you approach it with integrity and wisdom?

How can introspection guide you toward the path that aligns with your core values?

_____

_____

_____

_____

DAY 28:

SERVICE BEYOND
SELF

"We are born for cooperation, as are the feet, the hands, the eyelids, and the upper and lower jaws."

- Marcus Aurelius

Aurelius speaks to our innate nature to work collectively and serve others.

Meditation: Reflect on opportunities to aid others. How can you extend a helping hand?

How does serving others enrich your own journey?

_____

_____

_____

_____

DAY 29: TRIUMPH FROM TRIALS

"Out of difficulties grow miracles."

- Seneca, Letters, 12.7

Seneca illuminates the transformative power of challenges, shaping growth and resilience.

Meditation: Think back to a significant hurdle you've surmounted. What strengths did you discover within yourself?

How has that experience forged a deeper understanding of your capabilities and resilience?

_____

_____

_____

_____

DAY 30:
WISDOM FROM
WOUNDS

"Fire tests gold, suffering tests brave men."

- Seneca, De Providentia, 5.9

Seneca reminds us that only through trials will our character be strengthened.

Meditation: Reflect on a hardship you've faced. What lessons did it impart? How have these teachings shaped your understanding of life and fortified your spirit for future challenges?

_____

_____

_____

_____

_____

DAY 31:
GRACE IN GRIT

"Endure all things willingly, complaining of none, and the weight of your chains will be no more."

\- Epictetus, Discourses, 1.29

Epictetus speaks to the power of perspective, suggesting that our reactions determine the weight of our burdens.

Meditation: Consider a minor inconvenience you might face. How can you navigate it with grace and patience? How does changing your reaction transform the nature of the challenge?

_____

_____

_____

_____

_____

DAY 32:

BRAVELY FACING

CHALLENGES

"The greater the obstacle, the more glory in overcoming it."

- Seneca, Moral Letters, 76.3

Seneca emphasizes the transformative power of confronting daunting challenges head-on.

Meditation: Picture a significant, looming challenge. How would you approach it with determination and courage? How does visualizing your perseverance and eventual triumph bolster your confidence and resolve for real-life adversities?

_____

_____

_____

_____

DAY 33:

INNER FORTITUDE

"The strength of the soul grows in proportion as you subdue the flesh."

- Epictetus, Discourses, 4.9

Epictetus illuminates the boundless power and resilience of the human spirit.

Meditation: Reflect on moments where your inner strength prevailed. How can you tap into that deep reservoir of fortitude daily?

_____

_____

_____

_____

_____

_____

DAY 34: PERSEVERANCE PREVAILS

"Often it is tenacity, not talent, that rules the day."

— Seneca, Letters, 91.20

Seneca highlights the unparalleled value of persistence in the face of adversity.

Meditation: Think of a time you defied the odds through sheer determination. What drove you to persist?

How has that experience instilled a deeper sense of resilience?

_____

_____

_____

_____

DAY 35:

OBSTACLES AS

OPPORTUNITIES

"The impediment to action advances action. What stands in the way becomes the way."

- Marcus Aurelius, Meditations, 5.20

Aurelius proposes that challenges, instead of hindering us, can pave the path forward.

Meditation: Reflect on a challenge that spurred personal growth. How did it reshape your perspective?

How can you view life's hurdles as catalysts for growth?

_____

_____

_____

_____

DAY 36:
EPIPHANIES OF
ENLIGHTENMENT

"Wisdom is the oneness of mind that guides and permeated all things."

- Seneca

Seneca speaks of the profound impact wisdom can have on our lives, guiding our choices and perceptions.

Meditation: Recall a piece of wisdom that profoundly influenced your journey. How did it alter your path or perspective?

_____

_____

_____

_____

_____

DAY 37: GUIDED BY GREATNESS

"We should hunt out the helpful pieces of teaching and the spirited and noble-minded sayings which are capable of immediate practical application."

- Seneca, Letters, 33.11

Seneca emphasizes the transformative power of guidance from wise souls.

Meditation: Reflect on a mentor who left a lasting imprint on your life. What vital lessons did they impart?

_____

_____

_____

_____

DAY 38:

THE QUEST FOR

KNOWLEDGE

"Begin at once to live and count each separate day as a separate life."

- Seneca

Seneca encourages embracing every day as an opportunity for growth and discovery.

Meditation: What is something you've always wanted to learn? How can you take steps today to embark on this new journey?

_____

_____

_____

_____

_____

DAY 39:
SHARING WISDOM

"As the soil, however rich it may be, cannot be productive without cultivation, so the mind without culture can never produce good fruit."

- Seneca, Letters, 88.20

Seneca stresses the importance of nurturing the mind and sharing its fruits.

Meditation: Envision imparting wisdom to a younger individual. How can you share your experiences or knowledge to enlighten others and help the world?

_____

_____

_____

_____

_____

DAY 40:

THE JOURNEY OF

ENDLESS DISCOVERY

"Learning is an ornament in prosperity,
a refuge in adversity, and a provision in old age."

— Seneca, Letters, 58.30

Seneca celebrates the timeless value of knowledge, serving as an ally throughout life's phases.

Meditation: Reflect on your path of continual learning. What new skill or knowledge do you wish to pursue?

How can this quest not only enhance your life but also benefit those around you?

_____

_____

_____

DAY 41:
REVISIONS OF
REALITY

" To err is human, to persist [in the mistake] is diabolical."

- Seneca, Letters, 45.12

Seneca underscores the importance of recognizing mistakes and the growth that comes from rectifying them.

Meditation: Reflect on a past misconception you once held. How did you come to realize its inaccuracy? How can you prevent yourself from forming new misconceptions?

_____

_____

_____

_____

_____

DAY 42:

THE GATEWAY TO

INSIGHT

"Silence is a lesson learned through life's many sufferings."

- Seneca, Letters, 42.5

Seneca emphasizes the profound clarity and insight that can arise from silence.

Meditation: Spend a day immersed in silence. As thoughts surface, document them. This intentional silence offers a deeper understanding of your innermost thoughts, amplifies your insights and brings clarity to your mind's chatter.

_____

_____

_____

_____

DAY 43:
WALKING IN
ANOTHER'S SHOES

"Whenever you feel like criticizing anyone, just remember that all the people in this world haven't had the advantages that you've had."

- Seneca, Letters, 27.8

Seneca highlights the importance of empathy and understanding others' perspectives.

Meditation: Think of a recent interaction or disagreement. How might the situation appear from the other person's viewpoint?

_____

_____

_____

_____

DAY 44:

DISCERNING TRUTH

FROM PERCEPTION

"We suffer more in imagination than in reality."

- Seneca, Letters, 13.10

Seneca emphasizes the gap between objective facts and our subjective interpretations.

Meditation: Reflect on a recent situation. What were the indisputable facts, and what were your judgments or interpretations?

How can distinguishing between the two lead to clearer thinking and balanced reactions?

DAY 45:
A DAY WITHOUT
JUDGMENT

"Throw out your conceited opinions, for it is impossible for a person to begin to learn what he thinks he already knows."
                                        - Epictetus, Discourses, 2.17.1

Epictetus emphasizes the importance of an open mind, free from premature judgments.

Meditation: Embrace a day devoid of preconceived opinions to enhance your openness to new experiences and insights.

What new perspectives can you consider?

_____

_____

_____

_____

DAY 46: OBJECTIVITY OVER OFFENSE

"People are not disturbed by things, but by the views they take of them."

— Epictetus, Enchiridion, 1.5

Epictetus speaks to the power of perspective, emphasizing the freedom in not letting others' actions affect you.

Meditation: Reflect on a scenario where you might feel slighted.

How does maintaining objectivity provide emotional liberation and clearer understanding?

_____

_____

_____

_____

_____

DAY 47:

THE EBB AND FLOW

OF OPINIONS

"We are more often frightened than hurt; and we suffer more from imagination than from reality."

- Seneca, Letters, 13.11

Seneca underscores the fleeting and often baseless nature of opinions.

Meditation: Ponder the weight you give to others' opinions. How can you differentiate between objective truths and subjective views, allowing for a more authentic life?

_____

_____

_____

_____

DAY 48:
RE-EVALUATING
JUDGMENTS

"It is the power of the mind to be unconquerable."

- Seneca, Letters, 71.13

Seneca emphasizes the mind's ability to rethink, re-evaluate, and grow.

Meditation: Reflect on a judgment you've made in the past. With fresh eyes and a broader perspective, how might you reassess that viewpoint now?

_____

_____

_____

_____

_____

DAY 49:

THE PURSUIT OF UNDERSTANDING

"He who knows does not speak.
He who speaks does not know."

- Seneca, Letters, 42.10

Seneca emphasizes the value of listening and seeking comprehension over the desire to be heard.

Meditation: Consider a recent conversation or disagreement.

How might the outcome shift if you prioritized understanding the other person's perspective over asserting your own?

_____

_____

_____

_____

DAY 50:

DISTILLING LIFE'S

ESSENCE

"It is not that we have a short time to live, but that we waste a lot of it."

- Seneca, On the Shortness of Life, 1.1

Seneca nudges us to discern the truly significant from the fleeting, urging us to cherish what genuinely matters.

Meditation: Ponder the core pillars of your life. What truly holds meaning and value for you? How can you prioritize these essentials?

_____

_____

_____

_____

DAY 51:
LIBERATION IN
LIMITATION

"He who is brave is free."

- Seneca, Letters, 96.3

Seneca elucidates the freedom found in contentment and the courage to desire less.

Meditation: How might your life transform if you found contentment in having less?

How does embracing simplicity and curbing desires lead to a more liberated, fulfilled existence?

DAY 52:
SIMPLICITY IN SPACE

"Life is long if you know how to use it."

- Seneca, On the Shortness of Life, 2.5

Seneca speaks to the value of intentional living, including the spaces we inhabit.

Meditation: Consider a cluttered area in your living space. How might decluttering and creating a harmonious environment reflect and reinforce a harmonious mind?

_____

_____

_____

_____

_____

_____

DAY 53:

PURITY IN PAUCITY

"Nature's wants are slight; the demands of opinion are boundless."

- Seneca, Letters, 119.15

Seneca reminds us of the beauty in simplicity and the burdens of societal expectations.

Meditation: Imagine a life stripped of superfluities, focused only on the essentials.

How can adopting a minimalist approach in various aspects of life lead to a deeper appreciation of its true essence?

_____

_____

_____

_____

_____

DAY 54: SAVORING SIMPLICITY

"Wealth consists not in having great possessions, but in having few wants."

- Epictetus, Discourses, 2.7.4

Epictetus sheds light on the true nature of wealth, suggesting that contentment arises from simplicity rather than abundance.

Meditation: Reflect on the simple joys present in your life. What additional simplicities can you embrace and cherish?

_____

_____

_____

_____

_____

DAY 55:

SHEDDING EXCESS

"No person has the power to have everything they want, but it is in their power not to want what they don't have, and to cheerfully put to good use what they do have."

- Seneca, Letters, 123.3

Seneca speaks of the strength found in recognizing excesses and the freedom in letting them go.

Meditation: Reflect on a habit or indulgence that doesn't serve your highest good. How can you take steps to reduce or eliminate it for a more purposeful, contented existence?

_____

_____

_____

_____

_____

DAY 56:

LESS IS MORE

"It is quality rather than quantity that matters."

- Seneca, Letters, 94.5

Seneca emphasizes the richness found in savoring quality moments and experiences over the sheer volume of them.

Meditation: Today, aim to prioritize quality in all you do. If you often indulge in large meals, savor smaller, nourishing portions.

How does this shift in perspective enhance your appreciation and deepen your experiences?

_____

_____

_____

_____

_____

DAY 57:

THE EMBRACE OF EMPATHY

"Wherever there is a human being, there is an opportunity for kindness."

- Seneca, Letters, 9.10

Seneca highlights the universal potential for empathy and compassion in human interactions.

Meditation: Ponder the role empathy plays in your relationships and daily interactions.

How can intentional acts of kindness and a genuine desire to understand others enhance the quality of your connections?

_____

_____

_____

DAY 58:
WEAVING THE WEB
OF UNITY

"We are waves of the same sea, leaves of the same tree,
flowers of the same garden."

- Seneca, Letters, 65.12

Seneca speaks to the intrinsic interconnectedness of all life, emphasizing our shared essence.

Meditation: Reflect on the profound interconnection of all beings.

How can you foster a deeper sense of unity, embracing your role as a vital thread in the vast fabric of existence?

_____

_____

_____

DAY 59:

HEARING

IN THE SILENCE

"We have two ears and one mouth so that we can listen twice
as much as we speak."

- Epictetus, Enchiridion, 33.5

Epictetus underscores the importance and virtue of genuine listening over dominating a conversation.

Meditation: Reflect on a recent interaction. Were you truly present and attentive? Challenge yourself today to deeply listen to someone, absorbing their words without rushing to formulate a response.

How does this strengthen your bonds?

DAY 60:

A WORLD OF

EMPATHY

"We are all bound together... we are all in this together and we need to work together."

- Seneca, Letters, 71.13

Seneca speaks to the inherent unity of humanity and the power of collective compassion.

Meditation: Imagine a world where empathy is the prevailing force. How can embracing the idea of a global family inspire you to foster empathy in your daily life and contribute to this collective dream?

_____

_____

_____

_____

DAY 61:

UNSEEN STRUGGLES

"Be tolerant with others and strict with yourself."

- Marcus Aurelius, Meditations

Marcus Aurelius emphasizes the virtue of understanding towards others while holding oneself to rigorous standards.

Meditation: Reflect on a time someone treated you unfairly. Instead of harboring resentment, consider the possibility that they too might have experienced similar treatment or are grappling with their own challenges. How does this shift in perspective foster understanding and compassion, even in the face of adversity?

_____

_____

_____

_____

_____

DAY 62:

BRIDGING BROKEN

BONDS

"Begin each day by telling yourself: Today I shall be meeting with interference, ingratitude, insolence, disloyalty, ill-will..."
- Marcus Aurelius, Meditations

Marcus Aurelius prepares us for life's challenges, emphasizing understanding.

Meditation: Think of a strained relationship in your life. How can Stoic teachings guide you to approach reconciliation with understanding and patience?

_____

_____

_____

_____

DAY 63:
NATURE'S PEACEFUL EMBRACE

"Constantly regard the universe as one living being, having one substance and one soul."

\- Marcus Aurelius, Meditations

Aurelius speaks to the interconnectedness and tranquility found in nature.

Meditation: Ponder the serenity nature provides. How does immersing yourself in the natural world calm your spirit and offer a reprieve from life's chaos?

DAY 64:

NATURE'S WISDOM

"Look back over the past, with its changing empires that rose and fell, and you can foresee the future too."

— Marcus Aurelius, Meditations

Marcus Aurelius emphasizes the timeless lessons and cycles found in nature.

Meditation: Reflect on the simple contentment observed in creatures, from ants to elephants. Despite adversities, simplicity, and occasional lack, they find inner peace and joy.

What lessons can their simplicity and resilience offer you in your pursuit of genuine happiness?

_____

_____

_____

_____

DAY 65:
EMBRACING
TRUE LIFE

"Dwell on the beauty of life. Watch the stars and see yourself running with them."

\- Marcus Aurelius, Meditations Marcus

Aurelius emphasizes the rejuvenating power of nature and our place within it.

Meditation: Commit to spending time outdoors. As you immerse yourself in the natural world, notice its rhythm and harmony. How does connecting with nature ground you and offer a deeper appreciation for life's wonders?

_____

_____

_____

_____

DAY 66:

NATURE'S TRANQUIL EMBRACE

"Short-lived are both the praiser and the praised, and the rememberer and the remembered... All things are short-lived—this is their common lot."

- Marcus Aurelius, Meditations

Marcus Aurelius reminds us of the fleeting nature of life, urging us to find solace in the timeless embrace of nature.

Meditation: Imagine yourself enveloped in a tranquil natural setting, feeling the earth beneath and the sky above.

How does this visualization foster a deep connection with Mother Earth and offer a sanctuary from life's transience?

DAY 67:

MEDITATIVE SOLACE

"Look within.
Within is the fountain of good, and it will ever bubble up if
you will ever dig."

- Marcus Aurelius, Meditations

Aurelius emphasizes the inner wellspring of goodness, hinting at nature's ability to magnify this introspection.

Meditation: Seek a quiet outdoor spot for meditation. If it's winter, surround yourself with nature's visuals, be it videos, sounds, or potted plants. As you meditate, let nature amplify your inner reflections and cultivate inner peace. What secret thoughts surface in this state?

_____

_____

_____

_____

DAY 68:

EMBRACING LIFE'S

IMPERMANENCE

"Time is a river, a violent current of events, glimpsed once and already carried past us, and another follows and is gone."

— Marcus Aurelius, Meditations

Marcus Aurelius poetically speaks to the fleeting nature of time and all within it.

Meditation: Reflect on the changing seasons and the transient nature of every life form, including yourself. Recognizing this impermanence, how does it inspire you to live more fully, cherishing each moment?

_____

_____

_____

DAY 69:

CULTIVATING INNER

DISCIPLINE

"Discipline yourself to get what you want. Your desires won't be restrained, unless you do the restraining."

- Epictetus, Discourses, 3.12.8

Epictetus emphasizes the power of self-discipline in mastering desires and steering our life's course.

Meditation: Consider an area in your life that could benefit from greater discipline. What steps can you take to cultivate this discipline and align closer with your aspirations, ethics, virtues, and true self?

_____

_____

_____

_____

DAY 70:

FREEDOM THROUGH

MASTERY

"No man is free who is not master of himself."

\- Epictetus, Enchiridion, 14

Epictetus underscores the profound link between self-control and true freedom.

Meditation: Reflect on moments where exercising self-control granted you a deeper sense of freedom.

How can you cultivate self-control to experience even greater liberation in life?

DAY 71:

RESISTING THE

SIREN'S CALL

"He who reigns within himself and rules his passions, desires, and fears is more than a king."

- Marcus Aurelius, Meditations

Marcus Aurelius extols the virtue and strength found in mastering one's temptations.

Meditation: Identify a temptation that often sways you. Today, challenge yourself to resist its allure. Recognize the empowerment and inner strength that comes from such mastery. How does this exercise bolster your resolve for future challenges?

_____

_____

_____

_____

DAY 72:

MASTERING THE

INNER SELF

"You have power over your mind - not outside events. Realize this, and you will find strength."

- Marcus Aurelius, Meditations

Marcus Aurelius emphasizes the sovereignty we hold over our inner world and responses.

Meditation: Envision a life where external events don't dictate your reactions, but instead, you respond with calm and purpose.

How can you cultivate this inner strength in your everyday interactions?

_____

_____

_____

DAY 73:

INNER RESOLVE

"The happiness of your life depends upon the quality of your thoughts: therefore, guard accordingly, and take care that you entertain no notions unsuitable to virtue and reasonable nature."

— Marcus Aurelius

Aurelius speaks to the power of the mind and the strength in directing it towards virtue.

Meditation: Contemplate the depth of your willpower. Recall moments when your determination prevailed. How can you further hone this inner resolve to navigate challenges and align with your truest intentions?

_____

_____

_____

_____

DAY 74:
LESSONS IN
DISCIPLINE

"From every wrong, extract a right."

- Seneca

Meditation: Recall a past discipline lapse. What lesson emerged?

How can you harness this insight for future growth?

_____

_____

_____

_____

_____

_____

DAY 75:
POSITIVE RITUALS

"First say to yourself what you would be; and then do what you have to do."

- Epictetus

Meditation: Today, identify an area for improvement.

Establish a routine to cultivate this change and embrace growth.

_____

_____

_____

_____

_____

_____

_____

DAY 76: ENSHRINING A LEGACY

"What we do now echoes in eternity."

- Marcus Aurelius

Meditation: Ponder your desired legacy.

How will your actions today shape tomorrow's world?

Define your lasting impact.

_____

_____

_____

_____

_____

_____

DAY 77:
FAME VERSUS
ENDURING IMPACT

"Fame is something which must be won; honor, only something which must not be lost."

- Ancient Stoic wisdom

Meditation: Reflect on fame's fleeting nature compared to a lasting legacy.

What truly endures beyond fleeting accolades?

Define your deeper purpose.

_____

_____

_____

_____

DAY 78: PURPOSEFUL CONTRIBUTION

"He who does good to another does good also to himself."

- Seneca

Seek a good, charitable cause that resonates with your values.

How can you dedicate time, work, or resources to experience the fulfillment of purposeful giving?

_____

_____

_____

_____

_____

_____

_____

DAY 79:

ECHOES OF DEEDS

"Our actions may be impeded... but there can be no impeding our intentions or dispositions."

- Marcus Aurelius

Meditation: Imagine the ripple effect of your actions.

How do today's choices influence tomorrow's world?

Contemplate this lasting impact and how you can better align your actions with purposeful intention.

DAY 80:
EMBRACING
UNIVERSAL
CONNECTION

"We are all working together to one end, some with knowledge and design, and others without knowing what they do."

- Marcus Aurelius

Meditation: Reflect on your place within the vast cosmos. Feel the interconnectedness of all beings in this world. Recognize your role in the grand tapestry of existence and embrace the unity.

How can you better connect with others?

_____

_____

DAY 81:
SELFLESS ACTS OF
KINDNESS

"Our life is what our thoughts make it."

- Marcus Aurelius

Meditation: Recall a moment you acted selflessly, prioritizing another's well-being.

How did you feel?

Reflect on the impact and warmth of such deeds.

Let this memory inspire future acts of altruism.

_____

_____

_____

_____

DAY 82:

BEACON OF

INSPIRATION

"Associate with people who are likely
to improve you."

- Seneca

Meditation: How can your actions inspire those around you?

Seek opportunities to uplift your community and make a broader impact.

By embodying positive change, become a beacon for others, encouraging collective growth and unity.

_____

_____

_____

_____

DAY 83: EMBRACING ACCEPTANCE

"Accept whatever comes to you woven in the pattern of your destiny, for what could more aptly fit your needs?"

- Marcus Aurelius

Meditation: Reflect on a challenging aspect of your life. Contemplate its presence and consider embracing acceptance for inner tranquility. Recognize that sometimes, peace stems from acceptance rather than resistance.

How will you accept it with grace?

_____

_____

_____

_____

DAY 84:

THE LIBERATION OF

RELEASE

"Do not spoil what you have by desiring what you have not."

- Epicurus

Meditation: Consider the profound tranquility birthed from relinquishing attachments and desires.

Contemplate how releasing burdens and expectations can pave the way for genuine inner peace.

What burdens do you need to release right now?

_____

_____

_____

_____

_____

DAY 85:
LIBERATING
FORGIVENESS

"How much more grievous are the consequences of anger than the causes of it."

- Marcus Aurelius

Meditation: Today, challenge yourself to release a grudge. Understand the weight it carries and the peace that forgiveness can bring. Embrace the liberation of letting go.

What grudge is dragging you down and why? Is it really worth it? In the greater scope of life and history, was it really that bad?

How can you shift your perspective to willingly let it go?

_____

_____

DAY 86:

THE BURDEN OF

REGRETS

"Waste no more time arguing what a good man should be.
Be one."

Meditation: What regrets burden your heart and why? Recognize their weight and let them go.

Embrace the freedom of living in the present, unburdened by the past.

_____

_____

_____

_____

_____

DAY 87:

HARMONY WITH THE FLOW

"Nature does nothing in vain, and so whatever is, is for the sake of something else."

- Marcus Aurelius

Meditate on the natural rhythm and flow of life. How does it mirror the ebb and flow of your own existence?

Consider the interconnectedness of events and experiences.

Journal about how you can align more harmoniously with this universal flow in your daily life.

_____

_____

_____

_____

DAY 88:

LIBERATING FROM

RESENTMENTS

"Resentment is like taking poison and waiting for the other person to die."

- Marcus Aurelius

Meditation: What old hatreds are poisoning you? Challenge yourself to release old resentments and anger.

Reflect on the harm they cause and the inner peace that comes from letting go.

Embrace the freedom of forgiveness and understanding.

_____

_____

_____

_____

DAY 89:
EMBRACING LIFE'S
PURPOSE

"Fate leads the willing and drags along the reluctant."

- Seneca

Meditation: Reflect on a past event you resisted but now recognize its purpose.

How did this experience shape your path and contribute to your growth?

Acknowledge the wisdom in life's unfolding journey.

_____

_____

_____

_____

DAY 90:
AMOR FATI

"Let us train our minds to desire what the situation demands."

- Seneca

Meditation: Embrace the concept of "amor fati", the love of fate. Reflect on the idea that everything that has happened in your life has a bigger purpose beyond your current understanding.

How can you cultivate love and acceptance for all that life brings, recognizing it as an essential part of your journey?

_____

_____

_____

_____

_____

293

Conclusion

"Do every act of your life as though it were the very last act of your life."

- Marcus Aurelius

As we draw this book to a close, it's my heartfelt wish for each of you to embark on a life enriched with tranquility, strength, and fulfillment.

The path ahead won't always be easy, and it's the daily practice of these Stoic principles that will forge resilience in the face of adversity.

Remember, the pursuit of a virtuous life rests in your capable hands. It's a daily task, an hourly practice, a lifelong journey.

May you find profound wisdom in the simplicity of these teachings, allowing them to seep into your everyday actions, decisions, and thoughts. Let them bolster your courage, refine your perspectives, and bring a wellspring of joy and satisfaction that flows inward out.

As you step forward from this point, carry with you the certainty that you're equipped with timeless wisdom that has guided countless souls through the tempests of life.

May your days ahead be vibrant with the authentic happiness that comes from within, untouched by the chaotic sway of external forces.

Practice diligently, reflect deeply, and embrace the world with the steadfast spirit of a stoic.

Here's to a life not merely lived but lived with purpose, clarity, and an unshakeable peace within.

Bon voyage on your continuous journey through life's rich tapestry.

About the Author

Charles Abbott is an American writer with a passion for philosophy and social sciences based on human thought processes and behaviors. Abbott's writing is focused on personal development, mindset, and health in the modern world. He lives with his wife and two children in Austin, Texas.

Please Leave a 5-Star Review

If you enjoyed this book, please leave a positive review to help more readers discover Stoicism. Your review will help others because by applying the powerful Stoic principles, they too can lead happier lives.

"What we do now echoes in eternity."

\- Marcus Aurelius

Made in the USA
Coppell, TX
01 July 2024

34150702R00164